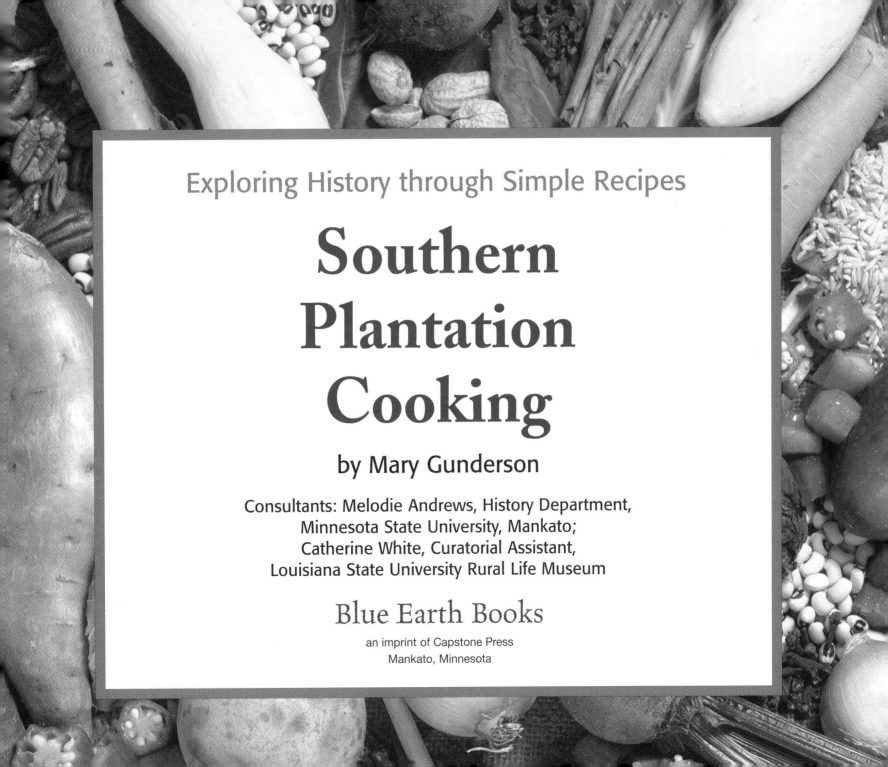

Exploring History through Simple Recipes

Southern Plantation Cooking

by Mary Gunderson

Consultants: Melodie Andrews, History Department,
Minnesota State University, Mankato;
Catherine White, Curatorial Assistant,
Louisiana State University Rural Life Museum

Blue Earth Books
an imprint of Capstone Press
Mankato, Minnesota

Blue Earth Books are published by Capstone Press
151 Good Counsel Drive, P.O. Box 669, Mankato, Minnesota 56002
http://www.capstone-press.com

6/07— Perma-Bound—$17.95

Library of Congress Cataloging-in-Publication Data
Gunderson, Mary.
    Southern plantation cooking / by Mary Gunderson.
    p. cm.—(Exploring history through simple recipes)
    Includes bibliographical references (p. 30) and index.
    Summary: Discusses the everyday life, family roles, cooking methods, most important foods, and celebrations of people on southern plantations before the Civil War. Includes recipes.
    ISBN 0-7368-0357-2
    1. Cookery, American—Southern style—History Juvenile literature. 2. Food habits—Southern States—History Juvenile literature. 3. Plantation life—Southern States—History Juvenile literature. [1. Cookery, American—Southern style—History. 2. Food habits—Southern States—History. 3. Plantation life.] I. Title. II. Series.
TX715.2.S68G86 2000
394.1'0975—dc21
                                                                                            99-27108
                                                                                            CIP

Editorial credits

Editors, Kerry Graves and Rachel Koestler; cover designer, Steve Christensen; interior designer, Heather Kindseth; illustrator, Linda Clavel; photo researcher, Kimberly Danger.

Acknowledgments

Blue Earth Books thanks the following children who helped test recipes: John Christensen, Matthew Christensen, Maerin Coughlan, Beth Goebel, Nicole Hilger, Abby Rothenbuehler, Alice Ruff, Hannah Schoof, and Molly Wandersee.
The author thanks Damon Lee Fowler and Susan Dosier for their assistance with this book.

Photo credits

Corbis/Bettmann, cover, 9; Gregg Andersen, cover (background) and recipes, 15, 17, 23, 27; Currier and Ives, 6-7; Archive Photos, 13, 16; North Wind Picture Archives, 14, 20, 28; American Stock/ Archive Photos, 18-19; Rudi Holnsteiner, 24, 26-27.

Editor's note

Adult supervision may be needed for some recipes in this book. All recipes have been tested. Although based on historical foods, recipes have been modernized and simplified for today's young cooks.

1 2 3 4 5 6 05 04 03 02 01 00

Contents

Cooking Help

Recipes

References

Metric Conversion Guide

U.S.	Canada
¼ teaspoon	1 mL
½ teaspoon	2 mL
1 teaspoon	5 mL
1 tablespoon	15 mL
¼ cup	50 mL
⅓ cup	75 mL
½ cup	125 mL
⅔ cup	150 mL
¾ cup	175 mL
1 cup	250 mL
1 quart	1 liter
1 ounce	30 grams
2 ounces	55 grams
4 ounces	85 grams
½ pound	225 grams
1 pound	455 grams

Fahrenheit	Celsius
325 degrees	160 degrees
350 degrees	180 degrees
375 degrees	190 degrees
400 degrees	200 degrees
425 degrees	220 degrees

Kitchen Safety

1. Make sure your hair and clothes will not be in the way while you are cooking.

2. Keep a fire extinguisher in the kitchen. Never put water on a grease fire.

3. Wash your hands with soap before you start to cook. Wash your hands with soap again after you handle meat or poultry.

4. Ask an adult for help with sharp knives, the stove, the oven, and all electrical appliances.

5. Turn handles of pots and pans to the middle of the stove. A person walking by could run into handles that stick out toward the room.

6. Use dry pot holders to take dishes out of the oven.

7. Wash all fruits and vegetables.

8. Always use a clean cutting board. Wash the cutting board thoroughly after cutting meat or poultry.

9. Wipe up spills immediately.

10. Store leftovers properly. Do not leave leftovers out at room temperature for more than two hours.

Cooking Equipment

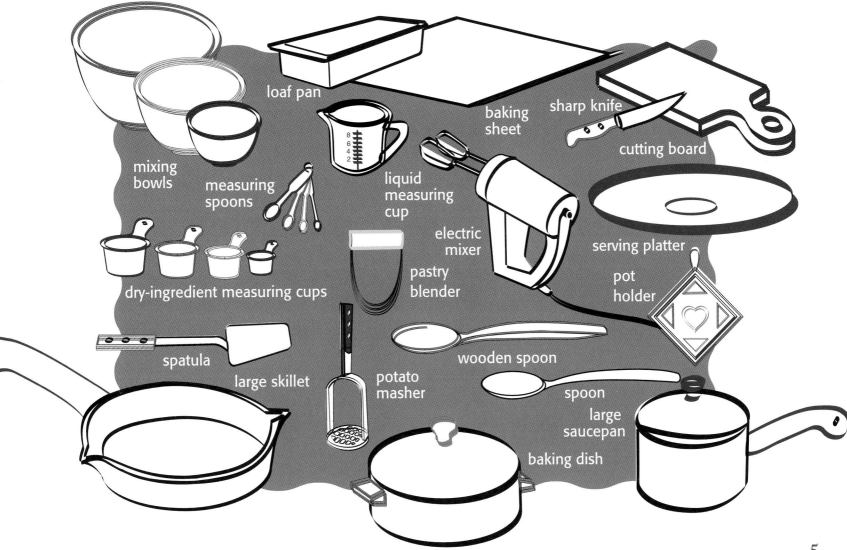

loaf pan

baking sheet

sharp knife

cutting board

mixing bowls

measuring spoons

liquid measuring cup

dry-ingredient measuring cups

electric mixer

pastry blender

serving platter

pot holder

spatula

large skillet

potato masher

wooden spoon

spoon

large saucepan

baking dish

Plantations in the United States

In the early 1600s, European settlers began to build plantations in the American colonies. Plantation owners established the first of these large farms in Virginia and Maryland. They grew tobacco and indigo for sale in Europe. These crops were very profitable for plantation owners. As they earned more money, the owners expanded their plantations. Owners needed many workers to grow the crops.

Not all Europeans who wanted to sail to the colonies could afford to pay their own passage. Plantation owners offered these people free passage to the colonies plus food and shelter when they arrived. In return, the people became indentured servants. They promised to work for the plantation owner with no salary for four to seven years. At that time, anyone who bought passage to Virginia received 50 acres (20 hectares) of land. The land allotted to indentured servants belonged to the plantation owner. In this way, plantation owners enlarged their farms and gained workers at the same time.

In the late 1600s, there was a shortage of indentured servants coming to the colonies. Plantation owners still needed many workers to tend their crops. In 1690, slave traders began to bring 10,000 Africans to the colonies every year. Many of these Africans were kidnapped, chained, and taken from their homeland forever. The

African slaves worked long hours picking cotton. In 1793, Eli Whitney invented a cotton gin that separated cotton fibers from their hulls and seeds. This machine and slave labor helped bring plantation owners large profits, making cotton "king" in the South.

wealthy plantation owners could afford to buy Africans to work in their fields and homes.

By the early 1800s, owners had built plantations throughout the southern United States. The warm climate allowed owners to grow many crops. Certain crops grew best in particular geographic regions. In South Carolina and Georgia, plantations produced rice in flooded fields. Cotton thrived in large inland fields from South Carolina through Texas. Planters raised sugar cane along the Mississippi River from Tennessee to Louisiana. Tobacco flourished on inland fields in Maryland, Virginia, and Kentucky.

Plantations were the most important businesses in the South until the Civil War (1861-1865). When fighting began, many Southern men and boys left the plantations and joined the Confederate Army to fight Union soldiers. Some Southern families had to leave their homes to escape battles. Slaves ran away and sometimes joined Northern armies to fight for their freedom. Crops died from neglect. In an effort to end the war, Union soldiers destroyed farm equipment, burned plantation homes, and stole livestock. Owners spent years rebuilding their plantations after the war.

Slavery became illegal after the North won the Civil War. Some African Americans worked as paid laborers on plantations. Most Southern African Americans became sharecroppers. They lived and worked on a plantation owner's land and were paid a share of the crops instead of wages.

KEY
- ☐ Free State or Territory
- ☐ Slave State or Territory
- ☐ Undecided Territories

Slave States and Free States, 1850

Oregon Territory

Minnesota Territory

Wisconsin

Michigan

unorganized territory

New Hampshire
Vermont

Maine

New York

Massachusetts

Rhode Island

Connecticut

New Jersey

Pennsylvania

Iowa

Ohio

Delaware
Maryland

Utah Territory

Indiana

Illinois

Virginia

California

Missouri

Kentucky

North Carolina

Tennessee

South Carolina

New Mexico Territory

Indian Territory

Arkansas

Pacific Ocean

Georgia

Mississippi

Alabama

Atlantic Ocean

Texas

Louisiana

Florida

Gulf of Mexico

Plantations and Slavery

Plantations depended on cheap labor. Buying and enslaving Africans was less expensive than hiring workers or keeping indentured servants. But Africans did not agree to work for plantation owners. Slave traders forced people to leave their homes in West Africa. Slave traders chained these Africans and brought them to the colonies by ship. Thousands of Africans died during the ocean journey.

Slave traders stopped bringing enslaved people from West Africa in 1808. But plantation owners continued to buy, sell, and trade American-born Africans. While some owners allowed enslaved people to work for their freedom, most did not.

By the 1780s, many people in the United States opposed slavery, especially in

the Northern states. By 1804, many Northerners had ended slavery in their states. Some Southern abolitionists also wanted to end slavery, but most plantation owners opposed this idea. The owners were rich and powerful. Many owners also were politicians who passed laws to strengthen slavery. The number of African slaves in the South grew from 650,000 in 1790 to nearly 4 million by the start of the Civil War in 1861.

The Plantation

Large plantations had many buildings. Houses, farm buildings, churches, and cemeteries all were built on a plantation. Plantations located far from towns sometimes had a school for the children of plantation owners.

The owner's home was the largest building on the plantation. Everyone called the home the "big house." The big house had bedrooms, a dining room, a study, a parlor or sitting room, and sometimes a ballroom. Long, roofed porches, or verandahs, surrounded many plantation houses. Plantation houses, like all other houses at this time, did not have indoor bathrooms. Outhouses stood behind the big house.

Plantation owners built the kitchen away from the big house. A cooking fire burned all day long in the kitchen's large fireplace. Stray sparks easily started fires. Separating the hot kitchen from the main house kept the big house cooler. The kitchen's location also kept the noise of cooking activity from interrupting life in the big house.

The kitchen building, pantry, dairy, icehouse, and smokehouse were located in the kitchen yard. In the dairy, slaves made milk into cream, butter, buttermilk, and sour cream. The owner stored ice in sawdust in the icehouse to keep food cold. Slaves preserved meats in the smokehouse. They covered pork with salt and then slowly cooked the meat over very low heat.

Farm buildings stood beyond the kitchen yard. The barn housed dairy cows, beef cattle, and hogs. Crop buildings might include a sugar house for making sugar cane into sugar and molasses, a ginning house for cleaning cotton, and a barn for drying tobacco. The blacksmith or carpenter buildings stood in this same area.

The overseer's house stood between the farm buildings and the slave quarters. The overseer managed the field slaves. His house was nicer than the slave quarters but not as fancy as the big house.

The slave quarters were a separate community within the plantation. Families crowded into small cabins. Slave quarters often included a dining hall and a sick house. The slaves also had their own cemetery.

Beyond all the buildings on the plantation were the fields. Plantation owners could own thousands of acres of land for their crops. Most of the owner's slaves worked 12 to 14 hours a day in the fields. Much of slaves' work was tiresome and hard physical labor. The overseer supervised them at all times.

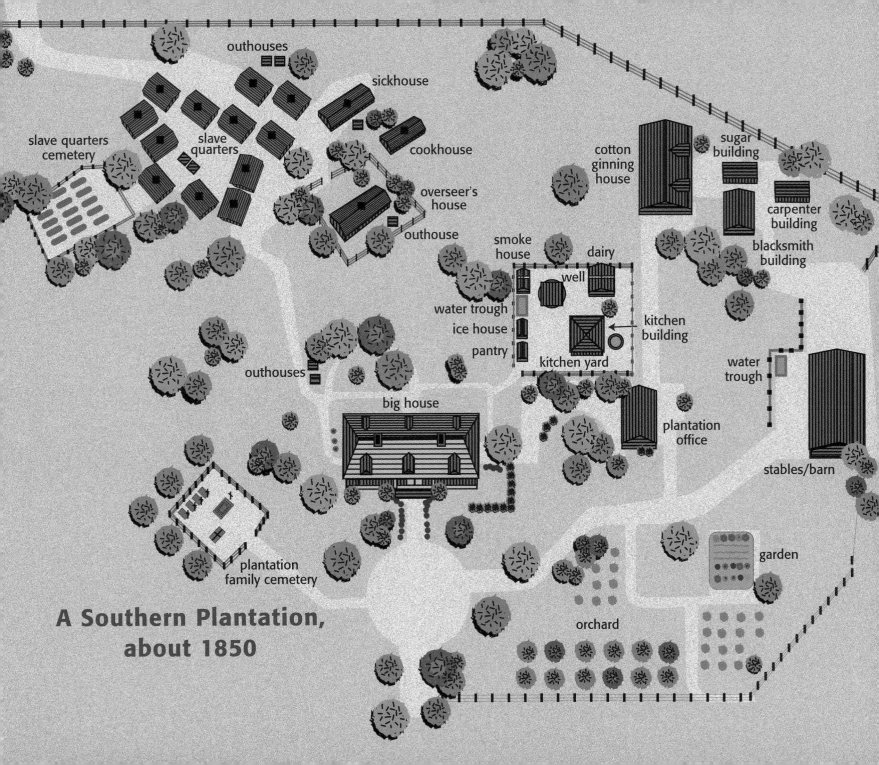

A Southern Plantation, about 1850

outhouses

sickhouse

slave quarters cemetery

slave quarters

cookhouse

overseer's house

outhouse

cotton ginning house

sugar building

carpenter building

blacksmith building

smoke house

dairy

well

water trough

ice house

pantry

kitchen building

kitchen yard

water trough

outhouses

big house

plantation office

stables/barn

plantation family cemetery

garden

orchard

Feather-light Buttermilk Biscuits

Slave cooks made biscuits for almost every meal. "Cathead" biscuits were about the size of a cat's head. The cooks sometimes punched or beat the dough with a mallet or the end of an ax for 15 to 30 minutes for beaten biscuits. Beaten biscuits baked into a stiff cracker. Slave cooks mixed buttermilk or cream into biscuit batter. These ingredients made biscuits light and delicious.

Ingredients
2 cups all-purpose flour
2 teaspoons baking powder
½ teaspoon salt
6 tablespoons cold butter
¾ cup buttermilk
¼ cup buttermilk, if needed
1 tablespoon butter or margarine
  for greasing

Equipment
medium bowl
dry ingredient measuring cups
measuring spoons
wooden spoon
pastry blender or 2 sharp knives
liquid ingredient measuring cup
fork
paper towel or napkin

baking sheet
spoon
pot holder
spatula

1. Preheat oven to 400°F.
2. In medium bowl, combine 2 cups flour, 2 teaspoons baking powder, and ½ teaspoon salt. Stir lightly to mix.
3. Add 6 tablespoons butter. With a pastry blender or two knives, cut butter into mixture until it is divided into pieces the size of peas.
4. Form a hole in the center. Add ¾ cup buttermilk all at once. Stir with fork just until dough is moistened, stirring completely from bottom to top. If dough seems dry, add more buttermilk, 1 tablespoon at a time, stirring once or twice after each addition. Be careful to not overstir. Overstirring makes biscuits tough.
5. Use a paper towel or napkin dabbed with 1 tablespoon butter or margarine to lightly grease baking sheet.
6. Drop 8 to 10 spoonfuls of dough on baking sheet. Bake for about 20 minutes. Serve immediately with butter, jam, gravy, sorghum syrup, or honey. These biscuits are best when eaten hot.

Makes 8 to 10 biscuits

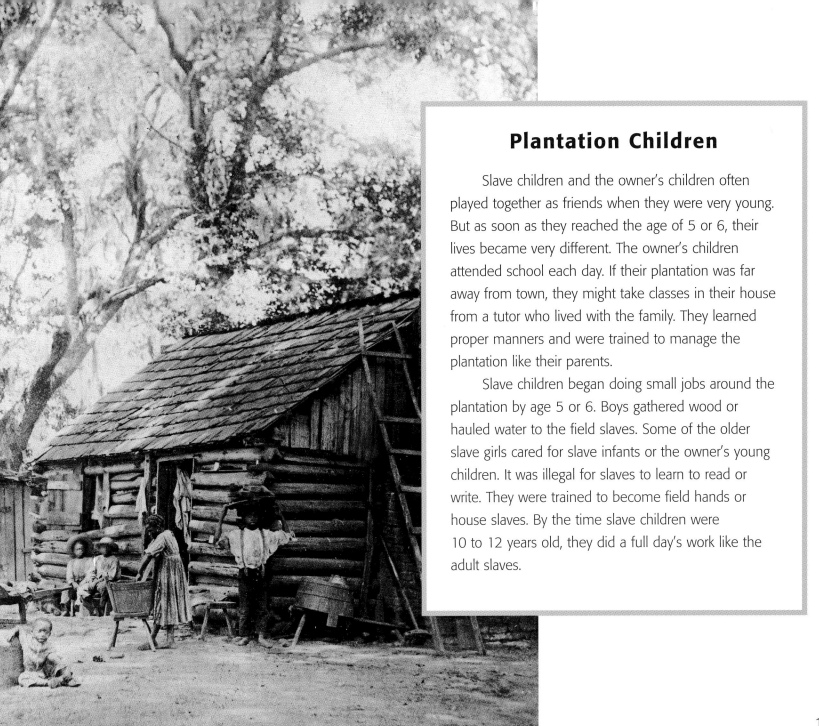

Plantation Children

Slave children and the owner's children often played together as friends when they were very young. But as soon as they reached the age of 5 or 6, their lives became very different. The owner's children attended school each day. If their plantation was far away from town, they might take classes in their house from a tutor who lived with the family. They learned proper manners and were trained to manage the plantation like their parents.

Slave children began doing small jobs around the plantation by age 5 or 6. Boys gathered wood or hauled water to the field slaves. Some of the older slave girls cared for slave infants or the owner's young children. It was illegal for slaves to learn to read or write. They were trained to become field hands or house slaves. By the time slave children were 10 to 12 years old, they did a full day's work like the adult slaves.

Life in the Big House

Everyone on the plantation had different duties. The owner kept track of the plantation's finances. He planned which crops to plant and assigned tasks to the overseer. The owner's wife, called the mistress, supervised much of the plantation's daily activity. She planned the meals and assigned the household work. She ran the plantation whenever her husband traveled.

A plantation mistress had many responsibilities. Each day, the mistress planned meals and checked on the amount of stored food. She gave the cook the ingredients to be used for each meal. She ordered supplies. The mistress supervised and helped make clothing for everyone on the plantation. In her free time, she wrote letters, sewed, tended her flower garden, or played the piano. Slave labor made it possible for her to enjoy hobbies.

Household slaves began to work before sunrise. Each day, they helped the owner and his family dress. They cared for the owner's young children. The slaves cooked and served meals, made beds, and cleaned the house. Every week, slaves washed, ironed, and mended clothes and bedding. Some slaves canned food, preserved meat, and made candles and soap. Others tended the vegetable garden.

During summer meals, slaves often fanned the family to keep them cool. Slaves sometimes used hand-held fans. Many slaves pulled a rope attached to a large wooden fan that hung over the table. Pulling the rope caused the fan to swing back and forth and send a breeze across the table.

Shrimp Creole over Rice

Ingredients

1 large onion
1 celery stalk
½ green pepper
2 tablespoons vegetable oil
1 tablespoon all-purpose flour
1 bay leaf
½ teaspoon dried thyme
½ teaspoon salt
¼ teaspoon ground black pepper
¼ teaspoon red (cayenne) pepper
1 can (14 ounces) diced tomatoes,
  undrained

2 cups chicken broth
1 tablespoon fresh lemon juice
1 tablespoon finely chopped parsley
1 pound (.5 kilogram) fresh or
  frozen shrimp
Hot cooked rice, about 3 cups

Equipment

cutting board
sharp knife
large saucepan
measuring spoons
liquid measuring cup
wooden spoon

1. Cut away top and bottom of onion. Peel outer papery layers. Slice onion into ¼-inch (.6-centimeter) slices. Chop slices into ½-inch (1.3-centimeter) pieces.
2. Trim celery stalk, on bottom and top, reserving fresh green leaves. Slice stalk into 2 or 3 long slices. Chop stalk and leaves into ½-inch (1.3-centimeter) pieces.
3. Cut green pepper in half. Cut out stem and remove seeds. Refrigerate one half. Cut remaining half in ½-inch (1.3-centimeter) cubes.
4. In large saucepan, heat 2 tablespoons vegetable oil over medium heat. Stir in onions. Cook until onions are tender, about 5 minutes. Stir in celery and green pepper. Cook about 3 minutes. Remove saucepan from heat.
5. Stir in 1 tablespoon flour, 1 bay leaf, ½ teaspoon salt, ½ teaspoon thyme, ¼ teaspoon black pepper, and ¼ teaspoon red pepper. Red pepper is spicy. If you do not like spicy food, add just a pinch between your thumb and forefinger.
6. Return to medium heat and cook about 1 minute, stirring constantly until mixture has thickened slightly.
7. Stir in tomatoes, 2 cups chicken broth, 1 tablespoon lemon juice, and 1 tablespoon parsley. Bring to a boil. Reduce heat to low. Cook about 10 minutes, stirring occasionally. Add shrimp. Cook about 20 minutes. Remove bay leaf. Serve over hot cooked rice.

Makes 6 to 8 servings

Life in the Slave Quarters

Slaves went home to the slave quarters after a long day's work in the house or field. The slaves could spend time with their families without being watched by the overseer or the plantation owner.

Many slave houses were small, one-room log cabins with a fireplace for cooking and heating. Some cabins were crude huts. The cabins had dirt floors and small windows, usually without glass. Cabins were cold and drafty in the winter and hot in the summer.

An average of five or six slaves lived together in each cabin. Slaves slept on cornhusk- or straw-filled mattresses.

Slaves had little control over their lives. They called their owners "master." Masters often changed slaves' African names to English names. Slave owners often sold slave children at a young age. Many of these children never saw their parents again.

Slaves led very difficult lives. They worked six days a week. Sunday was their only day off. Masters often whipped or sold slaves who complained. Slaves who tried to run away from their owners were severely punished. Some masters beat slaves so hard that the slaves died. Slave owners were not punished for killing their slaves.

The master chose the slaves' food. Most slaves did not have enough food to eat. Each week slaves received small amounts of milk, cornmeal, pork, and sometimes molasses. Slaves often received spoiled or unwanted meat. Pigs' feet, intestines, and skins were typical slave rations. Slaves used spices to make food taste better.

Many owners fed their slaves from a cookhouse. On some plantations, slave women cooked for their families in their cabins. Many slave women had one cooking pot and a single spoon for stirring. They had to be creative with food to feed the whole family with their limited rations. The women often made coosh-coosh. This fried dish is made with cornmeal, onions, and peppers. Slaves also fried or simmered the leafy tops of turnips or collard greens. Children ate a mixture of cornbread and pot likker. Pot likker was the leftover water from boiling greens or vegetables.

A slave woman sometimes baked ash cakes on Sunday. To make ash cakes, she mixed oat or wheat flour with buttermilk and lard. She scraped aside the hot ashes from the fire and dropped the dough on the fireplace floor. After the outer crust had baked dry, she covered the cake with the hot ash. The ash helped the batter rise as it baked.

Slaves often had their own small gardens. The slaves' gardens contained some of the foods introduced to America from Africa. The slave traders who brought slaves to North America also brought African plants. African slaves taught plantation owners how to grow and cook these foods, including okra, rice, and peanuts. They also raised eggplant, black-eyed peas, and sesame seeds. The slaves called sesame seeds benne (BEN-ee). They are still called benne in parts of the South today.

Oven-baked Okra

Ingredients
1 pound (.5 kilogram) fresh okra or
   1 package (10 ounces) frozen okra
1/3 cup white or yellow cornmeal
1 teaspoon salt
1 teaspoon pepper
2 egg whites
1 tablespoon butter or
   margarine for greasing

Equipment
cutting board
sharp knife

small bowl
dry-ingredient measuring cups
measuring spoons
wooden spoon
medium bowl
fork
paper towel or napkin
baking sheet
pot holder
spatula

1. Preheat oven to 350°F.
2. For fresh okra, trim ends and slice into 1/2-inch (1.3-centimeter) pieces. For frozen okra, let thaw slightly and break into pieces.
3. In small bowl, stir together 1/3 cup cornmeal, 1 teaspoon salt, and 1 teaspoon pepper.
4. In medium bowl, beat egg whites with fork until frothy. Toss okra in egg whites until well-coated.
5. Pour cornmeal mixture into okra mixture and stir until okra is well-coated.
6. Use paper towel or napkin dabbed with 1 tablespoon butter or margarine to lightly grease baking sheet.
7. Place okra in single layer on greased baking sheet. Bake for 12 to 15 minutes. Turn okra with spatula. Bake for an additional 15 minutes or until okra is golden brown and crisp.

Makes 6 to 8 servings

When the Dinner Bell Rang

Everyone on the plantation stopped to eat at midday. When the dinner bell rang, slaves in the fields ate small packages of cornbread and salt pork. Slave women prepared these foods at night for their families. Field workers also made hoe cakes by baking cornmeal and water over a fire on the blades of their work hoes. Slaves had only a short break to eat dinner.

Dinner was the largest meal of the day for the owner's family. Children returned from school for dinner. The mistress stopped her work in the house or garden. The plantation owner came in from the fields or left his office. The family gathered around the dining room table, and the slaves served the meal. Some mistresses required their slaves to whistle while they carried trays of food to the dinner table. They thought a whistling slave could not take a bite of food. Most masters did not allow their slaves to eat the same food as the family.

The slave cook and her helpers spent hours preparing a variety of dishes for dinner. Meals started with soup. The family then had a choice of meats. Dinner usually centered around ham, bacon, or other kinds of pork. Fried chicken also became a Southern specialty. Slaves served sweet potatoes, mashed potatoes and gravy, vegetables, salads, and pickles. Family members reached for hot biscuits and cornbread.

For dessert, they ate cake filled with whipped cream and topped with fresh peaches. Families ate pies made with apples, squash, pumpkin, or egg custard. They sometimes had fresh fruit for dessert. Ice cream was a rare treat. The family drank spring water, homemade cider, sweet milk, buttermilk, or coffee with cream and sugar.

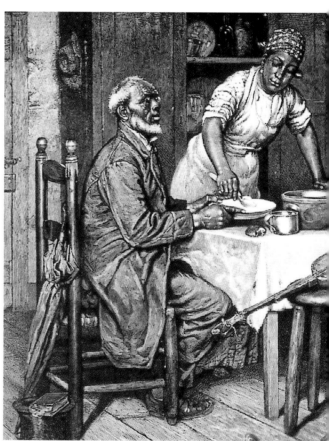

Some slaves ate the evening meal in their cabins. The cabin in this illustration is more elaborate than typical slave cabins.

Fried Chicken

Every Southern cook had a special recipe for fried chicken. Some cooks soaked chicken pieces in buttermilk. Other cooks fried chicken in hot lard. This recipe makes a crisp crust and tender meat without using much oil for cooking.

Ingredients

2 pounds cut-up chicken breasts, wings, legs, thighs or combination
½ cup all-purpose flour
¼ cup white or yellow cornmeal
1 teaspoon salt
1 teaspoon dried basil
½ teaspoon paprika
½ teaspoon pepper
1 tablespoon vegetable oil
1 tablespoon butter

Equipment

paper towels
1-gallon sealable plastic bag
dry-ingredient measuring cups
measuring spoons
large non-stick skillet
fork or tongs

1. Rinse and pat chicken dry with paper towels. Leave skin on for crispier chicken.
2. In a 1-gallon plastic bag, combine ½ cup flour, ¼ cup cornmeal, 1 teaspoon salt, 1 teaspoon basil, ½ teaspoon paprika, and ½ teaspoon pepper.
3. Place one chicken piece at a time into bag with flour mixture. Seal bag and shake until chicken is coated with flour mixture. Repeat until all pieces have been floured.
4. Heat 1 tablespoon oil and 1 tablespoon butter in skillet until butter is melted. Carefully and gently, add chicken to skillet.
5. Brown chicken in skillet, turning with fork or tongs. Be careful not to pierce skin. Juices may run out and chicken will become tough. Continue browning until all sides are brown, about 10 minutes.
6. Remove skillet from heat. Reduce heat to medium-low. Return pan to heat and cook about 20 minutes, uncovered, turning chicken every 4 to 5 minutes. Serve immediately with feather-light buttermilk biscuits for a traditional Southern meal.

Makes 6 to 8 servings

Plantation Hospitality

Plantation families often entertained guests. They treated their guests with affection and generosity. A family's hospitality showed its good manners and its place in society. The pineapple was a symbol of hospitality on southern plantations. Many plantation owners had pineapple designs carved into furniture and woodwork.

Plantation families entertained for weddings, funerals, balls, and horse races. Friends or relatives sometimes arrived for a meal or for a short visit. Other guests came from long distances and stayed for days or weeks. These guests brought their own slaves to help with chores. Visitors provided a welcome change from the plantation family's daily routine. Guests brought news from the world outside the plantation.

Plantation dinner parties were very elaborate. The meal had many courses. Guests were not expected to sample every food offered to them. They could pick their few favorite dishes. Slaves removed all dishes and wiped off or replaced the tablecloth between courses.

The mistress selected main dishes of chickens, duck, partridge, quail, pheasants, and pigeons. She also chose dishes made from pork, beef, veal, mutton, and venison. On plantations near the ocean, mistresses often selected fresh shrimp, clams, oysters, and crab for the main dishes.

Dessert often was the highlight of the meal. Plantation owners might offer up to 20 different desserts. Guests chose from cobblers, pies, puddings, layer cakes, or pound cakes with strawberries.

After meals, slaves served guests fruit and nuts with a dessert wine or brandy.

Pound Cake with Strawberries

Ingredients

1 cup butter
1 3/4 cups sugar
5 eggs
2 teaspoons vanilla
2 cups all-purpose flour
2 teaspoons baking powder
1/2 teaspoon salt
3/4 cup buttermilk
1 tablespoon butter or
   margarine for greasing

1 pint strawberries
1/4 cup sugar
whipped cream

Equipment

2 medium bowls
dry-ingredient measuring
   cups
electric mixer or hand mixer
measuring spoons

liquid measuring cups
paper towel or napkin
loaf pan, 9 inches by
   5 inches (23 centimeters
   by 13 centimeters)
cutting board
sharp knife
small bowl
spoon
wooden toothpick
pot holder

For pound cake:

1. Preheat oven to 325°F.
2. In medium bowl, mix 1 cup butter and 1 3/4 cups sugar at medium-high speed until mixture is smooth.
3. Add 5 eggs and 2 teaspoons vanilla. Beat at medium speed until thoroughly mixed.
4. In another bowl, combine 2 cups flour, 2 teaspoons baking powder, and 1/2 teaspoon salt.
5. Add 1 cup flour mixture and 1/4 cup buttermilk to egg mixture while beating at low speed. Add remaining flour mixture and remaining 1/2 cup buttermilk. Continue beating just until batter is smooth. Overstirring will make cake tough.
6. Use paper towel or napkin dabbed with 1 tablespoon butter or margarine to lightly grease bread loaf pan.
7. Pour batter into pan. Bake for 65 to 70 minutes or until toothpick inserted in center comes out clean. Prepare strawberry topping while cake bakes.
8. Remove from oven and cool cake in pan for 10 minutes. Loosen cake from sides with knife. Turn out on wire rack and cool completely. Serve cake slices with strawberries and whipped cream.

For strawberry topping:

1. Trim green tops and thinly slice strawberries.
2. Put strawberries into small bowl and sprinkle with 1/4 cup sugar. Stir until mixed. Let stand about 15 minutes.

Makes 12 servings

Orchards and Gardens

From March through early autumn, slaves planted, picked, and weeded the garden and orchards. The long growing season in the South gave families a large variety of produce. Gardens full of celery, squash, cauliflower, eggplant, cabbage, tomatoes, cantaloupes, and watermelons thrived during the hot, humid summers. Slaves tended rows of corn, black-eyed peas, string beans, lima beans, carrots, okra, and turnips. Slaves stored onions, potatoes, pumpkins, sweet potatoes, parsnips, and beets in the root cellar.

In early summer, slaves picked green corn. Families cut the corn from the cob and ate it mixed with cream. Plantation families ate ripe sweet corn in the fall. The slave cook dried ripened corn and ground it into cornmeal for biscuits and breads.

The cook and her helpers pickled cucumbers, watermelon rinds, peaches, beets, and apples. Each cook had her own recipes for chutneys, relishes, and chow-chows. These sauces, made from vegetables or fruit, were mixed with sugar, vinegar, and seasonings.

In the summer and fall, slaves picked ripe peaches, apples, mulberries, figs, cherries, and pears from orchard trees. Slaves preserved some of the fruits in sugar syrup and some as jams or jellies. Slaves often dried grapes for raisins or crushed grapes to make homemade wine or jelly.

Vegetables Well-done

Plantation families liked their vegetables well-cooked. They believed vegetables were easier to digest if they were very soft. The cook often began to boil vegetables for dinner right after breakfast. In plantation times, many people lost teeth when they were in their 30s. They found soft vegetables easier to chew.

The green vegetable shown here is okra. Okra was used in many Southern dishes and is still a popular vegetable in the South today.

Baked Yellow Squash with Onions

Ingredients

2 pounds yellow squash
2 large sweet onions
¼ cup butter, melted
1 teaspoon sugar
½ teaspoon salt
½ teaspoon pepper
1 tablespoon butter for greasing

Equipment

cutting board
sharp knife
paper towel or napkin
baking dish with cover or aluminum foil
small bowl
measuring spoons

1. Preheat oven to 350°F.
2. Trim ends of yellow squash and slice into ¼-inch (.6-centimeter) slices.
3. Cut away top and bottom of onions. Peel outer papery layers. Slice onion into ¼-inch (.6-centimeter) slices.
4. Use a paper towel or napkin dabbed with butter to lightly grease bottom and sides of baking dish.
5. Layer squash and onions in baking dish.
6. In small bowl, combine ¼ cup melted butter, 1 teaspoon sugar, ½ teaspoon salt, and ½ teaspoon pepper. Drizzle butter mixture over squash and onions.
7. Cover and bake for about 1 hour. Serve immediately.

Makes 6 to 8 servings

Puttin' up Pork

Most plantation families ate pork more than any other meat. Hogs were easy to raise. They grew quickly and could survive on many foods. Hogs ate kitchen scraps or found nuts and greens in the woods.

In December, plantation mistresses instructed slave men to kill the hogs. After the men killed the hogs, they scraped the bristles off the skin with a knife and set them aside to make into brushes. Some of the hogs' skin was saved to make saddles or small leather items.

The mistress, cook, and other slaves knew how to use every part of a hog. The owner's family ate ham, spareribs, bacon, and liver. Pickled pig's feet were a favorite food. The cook even used parts such as the snout, ears, brains, and tail. The cook scraped and cleaned the pig intestines. Later, she stuffed them with chopped meat to make sausage.

The mistress saved every bit of pork fat. Plantation cooks used this lard to cook and flavor foods. Cooks scraped the lard into a large pot and melted it. They poured the liquid through cloth into crocks. This method strained out the cooked bits of meat and gristle from the lard. They saved these bits to flavor other foods.

Mistresses helped fill the smokehouse with ham, sausage, bacon and other pork. The mistress often participated in this chore to prevent slaves from taking extra rations. The slaves then lit slow-burning fires in the smokehouse. They hung the salt-cured hams, bacon, and sausages in the smokehouse for days. The smoke dried and flavored the meats and kept them from spoiling.

Slaves received any meat that the master's family did not want. The mistress gave slaves the skin, jowls, and meat scraps called chitterlings that were scraped from the animal intestines. Slaves often ate the small meat bits strained from lard. The owner gave the slaves greasy scraps called "fatback" as part of their daily rations.

After the smokehouse was packed with pork, slaves lit a slow-burning fire in the fire pit. The mistress locked the door and left the meat to dry.

Country Ham with Red-eye Gravy

Ingredients	Equipment
1- to 1½-pound (.5- to .7-kilogram) ham, sliced about ¾-inch (1.9-centimeter) thick	cutting board sharp knife large skillet fork
⅓ cup water	serving platter or plate liquid measuring cup plastic spatula

1. Cut each ham slice into 6 pieces.
2. Heat skillet over medium-high heat. Add ham and reduce heat to medium.
3. Fry on one side 4 to 5 minutes, or until lightly browned. Turn and fry on other side another 4 to 5 minutes or until lightly browned.
4. Remove skillet from heat. Remove hot ham slices with fork and place on platter or plate to serve.
5. Return skillet to medium heat. Stir in ⅓ cup water. Use spatula to scrape crisp bits from bottom of pan. Be sure to use a plastic spatula. A metal spatula may damage the skillet.
6. Bring gravy to a boil. Reduce heat to low and cook about 1 minute. Serve immediately with fried ham.

Makes 4 to 6 servings

Christmas in the Big House

Plantation families and slaves spent weeks preparing for Christmas celebrations. The mistress made sure the slaves overfed the turkeys to fatten them for roasting. She set aside the best ingredients for holiday meals. Slaves repaired buildings and cleaned the big house from top to bottom. The owner's family decorated the big house with holly and evergreen branches, ribbons, and other ornaments. They prepared gifts for the family and the slaves.

The mistress invited friends and relatives for meals and parties. Some guests lived far away and visited only at Christmas. Everyone exchanged news of weddings, births, and deaths with one another. Formal meals, tea times, and dances provided entertainment throughout the season.

Christmas celebrations featured large meals with a variety of foods. Plantation families and their guests ate snacks between the meals. Slaves served special Christmas drinks like eggnog and syllabub. Syllabub was a drink of white wine with dollops of whipped cream that the adults enjoyed. Mistresses sometimes offered a light dessert to end the feasts. The slaves served ambrosia. This dish of orange slices layered with coconut is still served as a Christmas dessert in the South today.

On New Year's Day, the family and their guests sat down to a dinner of black-eyed peas cooked with ham hocks. This traditional food was said to bring good luck throughout the year. Everyone wished one another good health and continued wealth.

Plantation owners presented foods in a fashionable style to impress their guests. Guests ate from china bowls and plates imported from Europe.

Ambrosia

Ingredients
4 medium navel oranges
3 tablespoons powdered
  sugar
¾ cup coconut

Equipment
small bowl
medium serving bowl
measuring spoons
dry-ingredient measuring
  cups

1. Peel oranges over small bowl and separate each segment. Save any juice caught in the bowl.
2. Place orange segments into serving bowl. Toss gently with 3 tablespoons powdered sugar and ¾ cup coconut. Drizzle with orange juice in small bowl over mixture.
3. Refrigerate 30 minutes to 2 hours. Serve in clear glass bowls.

Makes 6 to 8 servings

Big Times in the Slave Quarters

Christmas was known as Big Times in the quarters. On some plantations, masters allowed slaves to celebrate Christmas as long as a Yule, or holiday, log burned. Slave men went to the woods in search of the largest, wettest tree stump they could find. The holiday began when they lit a smoldering fire under the stump. When the Yule log burned out, slaves said good-bye to relatives and ended their celebration.

Household slaves worked during the Christmas holidays. The cook and her helpers prepared food for the owner's guests. Slaves made beds, served meals, and cleaned up after parties. They hurried with their work so that they could join the celebration in the quarters.

During the holidays, some owners permitted their slaves to visit nearby plantations. Traveling slaves carried passes from their owners. Many husbands, wives, parents, and children saw each other only once each year at Christmastime.

Some plantation families invited slaves to come to the big house to receive gifts or to drink a glass of Christmas punch. The master and mistress sometimes visited the quarters. Their gifts usually were new clothing or shoes for the slaves. The master also might give out extra rations or better food than usual for the slaves to eat during the holidays.

Slaves prepared for their own celebrations. In the days before Christmas, mothers sewed special dresses and shirts from leftover material from the big house. Fathers gathered unwanted items from the owner's family to make dolls or toys for their children.

On many plantations, slaves gathered for Christmas dinner. Each woman brought her best one-pot dish. Some slave women roasted chicken and opossum or stewed rabbit in gravy. Others fried greens with salt pork. Men, women, and children enjoyed pans of pickled pig's feet, boiled cabbage, and baked squash. As a treat, slaves sometimes served sweet potato pie for dessert.

Sweet Potato Pie

The sweet potatoes for this recipe may be baked a day or two in advance and refrigerated.

Ingredients
2 medium sweet potatoes
¾ cup firmly packed brown sugar
3 eggs
¾ cup half-and-half
1 teaspoon cinnamon
½ teaspoon salt
½ teaspoon nutmeg
½ teaspoon ground ginger
¼ teaspoon cloves
1 unbaked 9-inch (23-centimeter) pie shell

Equipment
baking sheet
sharp knife
medium bowl
potato masher or fork
large bowl
dry-ingredient measuring cups
liquid measuring cup
measuring spoons
electric mixer or hand mixer
aluminum foil
pot holders

1. Preheat oven to 350°F.
2. Place sweet potatoes on baking sheet. Bake for about 1 hour. Do not turn off oven.
3. Cool sweet potatoes for 10 minutes. Peel by pulling strips of skin away from the flesh with a sharp knife.
4. Mash potatoes in medium bowl with potato masher or fork.
5. In large bowl or large mixer bowl, combine potatoes, ¾ cup brown sugar, 3 eggs, ¾ cup half-and-half, 1 teaspoon cinnamon, ½ teaspoon salt, ½ teaspoon nutmeg, ½ teaspoon ginger, and ¼ teaspoon cloves.
6. Beat at medium speed until smooth. Pour into pie shell. Bake for 50 to 55 minutes or until filling is set and a knife inserted in center comes out clean. If crust edges turn brown before pie is done, use pot holders to gently place strips of aluminum foil over crust edges and continue baking, as directed.

Makes 8 to 10 servings

Some slave couples married during Big Times. Slaves created broom jumping to honor their marriage unions. The broom symbolized the joining of two families. Other slaves held the broom to show their support for the couple. The couple then held hands and jumped over the broom into matrimony. Masters did not recognize slave marriages as legal.

Words to Know

abolitionist (ab-uh-LISH-uh-nist)—someone who worked to end slavery before the Civil War

chitterlings (CHIT-ur-lings)—the small intestines of animals, usually pigs; chitterlings were cleaned and simmered for eating or filled with meat.

cracklings (KRAK-lings)—the crunchy bits of meat and gristle strained from melted lard

emancipation (i-man-si-PAY-shuhn)—the act of freeing a person or group from slavery or control

hospitality (hoss-puh-TAL-uh-tee)—a generous and friendly way of treating guests

indigo (IN-duh-goh)—a plant that produces dark, purple berries; a dark blue dye is made from indigo.

lard (LARD)—the melted fat from pigs

mutton (MUHT-uhn)—the meat of a butchered sheep

overseer (OH-vur-see-uhr)—a person hired by the plantation owner to manage and direct the field slaves

root cellar (ROOT SEL-ur)—a cool, dark room below ground used to store vegetables and preserved foods

territory (TER-uh-tor-ee)—an area of the United States that is not yet a state

veal (VEEL)—the meat of a butchered calf

venison (VEN-uh-suhn)—the meat of a butchered deer

To Learn More

Bial, Raymond. *The Strength of These Arms: Life in the Slave Quarters.* Boston: Houghton Mifflin, 1997.

Dosier, Susan. *A Civil War Cookbook: The Confederacy.* Exploring History through Simple Recipes. Mankato, Minn.: Capstone Press, 2000.

Erickson, Paul. *Daily Life on a Southern Plantation, 1853.* New York: Lodestar Books, 1998.

Kent, Deborah. *African-Americans in the Thirteen Colonies.* Cornerstones of Freedom. New York: Children's Press, 1996.

McKissack, Patricia and McKissack, Frederick. *Christmas in the Big House, Christmas in the Quarters.* New York: Scholastic, 1994.

Places to Write and Visit

Ash Lawn-Highland
1000 James Monroe Parkway
Charlottesville, VA 22902

**Louisiana State University
    Rural Life Museum**
6200 Burden Lane
Baton Rouge, LA 70898

Middleton Place
4300 Ashley River Road
Charleston, SC 29414

Natchez Pilgrimage Tours
Canal Street Depot
P. O. Box 347
Natchez, MS 39120

**Tezcuco African-American
    Museum**
3138 Highway 44
Darrow, LA 70725

Waveland State Historic Site
225 Waveland Museum Road
Lexington, KY 40514

**Westville Living History
    Village**
1850 Martin Luther King
    Boulevard
P. O. Box 1850
Lumpkin, GA 31815

Internet Sites

Canadian Series of the North American Negro
http://www.niica.on.ca/csonan/startframe.htm

Louisiana Antebellum Homes Tour
http://www.fabt.com/tour.htm

Louisiana State University Rural Life Museum
http://rurallife.lsu.edu

Middleton Place
http://www.middletonplace.org

Westville Living History Village
http://www.westville.org

Index